SOMETHING I EXPECTED TO BE DIFFERENT

ALSO BY JOSHUA BECKMAN

Things Are Happening

SOMETHING I EXPECTED
TO BE DIFFERENT

✳

Joshua Beckman

Verse Press

ATHENS, GA   AMHERST, MA

Poems from this book first appeared in *American Poetry Review, Cello Entry, Harper's, The Massachusetts Review, Rhizome, Skanky Possum* and *The Works*. The author wishes to thank the editors of these publications and his family and friends who were his support while he wrote this book.

Published by Verse Press [www.versepress.org]

Library of Congress Cataloging-in-Publication Data
Beckman, Joshua.
    Something I expected to be different / Joshua Beckman. — 1st ed.
      p. cm.
    ISBN 0-9703672-4-4 (pbk. : alk. paper)
    I. Title.
    PS3552.E2839 S65 2001
    811'.54—dc21   00-013083

Set in Electra
Book design by Ben Tyler
Cover photograph by Joshua Beckman

Printed in the United States of America
9 8 7 6 5 4 3 2 1
First edition

CONTENTS

ODE TO THE AIR TRAFFIC CONTROLLER

Melbourne, Perth, Darwin, Townsville,
Belém, Durban, Lima, Xai-Xai planes
with wingspans big as high schools
eight hundred nine hundred tons a piece
gone like pollen, cumulus cirrus
altostratus nimbostratus people getting skinny
just trying to lose weight and the sky
the biggest thing anyone ever thought of
Acceptance, Vancouver, Tehran, Maui
school children balloons light blue nothing
one goes away not forever, in fact
most people, at least if you are flying
Delta, come down in Salt Lake City
Fairbanks, Kobe, Aukland, Anchorage
from Cleveland a hundred Hawaii-bound Germans
are coming in low, not to say too low
just low pull up Amsterdam pull up Miami
historically a very high-strung bunch
smokers eaters tiny planes must circle
we have bigger problems on our hands
New York, Tokyo, Hong Kong, Paris

---

the boy who has been ignoring dinner
throws thirteen paper planes out the window
does it look like this? Tashkent, Nome, Rio,
Hobart, yes yes it looks just like that
now do your homework Capetown Capetown
lots of rain good on one good on two
go three go four go five go six
Mau, Brak, Zella, Ghat, an African parade
good on two good on three
please speak English please speak English
good on five good on six gentlemen:
the world will let us down many times
but it will never run out of coffee
hooray! for Lagos, Accra, Freetown, Dakar
your son is on the telephone the Germans
landed safely Seattle off to Istanbul
tiny planes please circle oh tiny planes
do please please circle

LEAVE NEW YORK

Leave New York or the poem will kill you
Langston Hughes wrote $ $ $ to be black
and $ $ $ so, soaking soaking
"Sapwood posts are a little bit cheaper"...
"a little bit cheaper" just write it and
come to dinner, don't come to dinner
until you've written your poem "cheaper
than heartwood / I could" "I could
have bought all the heartwood from the start"
the startling thing is that they send a man off
into the woods with nothing, that a man with everything
sends off into the woods and once there
says, I have made terrible mistakes
with my life, branch redeem me, fallen
bird redeem me, I have spent on walkmen
others have folded my laundry, dry leaves
dry branches a great fire to cook
a meal for you is the cook's pleasure
to skimp out on the waitress is a shame
no matter how broke you are fall to your knees
in front of the kettle fire on Lafayette

and beg forgiveness of the Waitress God
this sort of calamity will not be remedied
without drama please burning city sooty cinders
please, six dollars for every shelf
we have spices and more spices
eight dollars a trash can
garbage and more garbage

I can smell your pancakes
and I will take them away from you.

We sent him out to ride the subway
he did and he returned
…"Men have anger about everything"
and the elders nod wisely "Men
have distrust about everything" and
the elders nod wisely "Men see nothing
in front but the toll and the timeline"
the elders nod wisely
                       wisely
     $$$$$$
             rattled
   through his dreams
  the subway is a dollar fifty
  and a dollar fifty is nothing
     the subway goes to Coney Island
     the subway goes to Jamaica
  the subway is so intricate
     the masses   the masses

You must leave us now to ride the subway
ride the subway leave us now, leaves are drying
leaves are falling, beautiful beautiful subway car
overground overground subway car, leave the city
and fall fall fall.

You are a dollar fifty
Rent stabilize the elders
Damn and praise the elders
Do not spend $39.00 on THE HAND OF THE POET
Do not spend $1.00 on two scallion pancakes
Do not spend a fortune on the body of adonis
Damn the gym and the vendor
                    the city and its commerce
Do not fill your house with useless crap
Do not escape on a motorcycle
            only to send rent checks back
Do not hail a ten dollar cab to blow off steam
            and smoke his back seat up
            and watch the meter jump by quarters
Do not spend $7.50 on AXE HANDLES by Gary Snyder
Do not spend $35.00 on the collected anyone
Do not e-mail yourself to the country from work
Do not bless the commuter train
            or the krishnas selling oatmeal
Volcano of poverty
    aftershock of small receipts
                pay out a quarter
                pay out a quarter
                pay out a quarter
            the next thing you're broke.

Gray building
between all the other buildings
suitcases on top of suitcases
on top of suitcases to the roof.
Climb and do not say I climb
reach the top and do not say
I have reached the top
accept the applause of the hot frying pan
as if it were the elders saying
we sent you out to the subway to the city
to the mean fatty world and we applaud
your success, and do not say I hear the elders,
I think I hear the elders.

WYOMING

Breath
a highway
a van full of tulips
moves through Wyoming
the wide way of the sky
becoming dark
soaked blackness
white van speeding along
the very bottom of the world
with purpose and though it seems tiny
seems delicate fabricated hope
hope's motor even pressing on through nothing
is a man age forty-two
his slight boy in tow
ear to the aluminum floor
the crushed pavement beneath
a white van turning to grayness
to gone its sure propulsion
its low beams its flowery bulk
past towns simple some sort of
bowl full of beautiful

bulbous yellow things half a dozen
apples bumping around
is what created the universe
dark and through it a van pushes
tulipless night falling away and saying
at night a van full of tulips
moves nightly through Wyoming
is also to say that a van
is propelled without will
without likeliness into the world
a man within it
as flowers are within it
cooperative and dark
driving drinking coffee
keeping himself awake
for lengths of time
slowing at the sight of towns
their growing glow
from earth's flattened field
here and forever is how long
he imagines he will drive
this van full of tulips because driving
this sort of van even late at night
even for ten hours at a time
is not that hard is almost easy
its low beams its flowery bulk
past towns where there will always be
folks on the verge of things needing tulips
to celebrate with when they celebrate
they will want them perched on tables
and opening up on tables in towns

the way towns perch and open
on empty sand as if pop-up
surprise flowers decorating
the nowhere tabletop of the world
the suggestion of people in restaurants
their empty tables pulling him
yet nothing so fine as a nap
on the side of the road
as your seat belt
when it is off and you fall across
both seats the blessing
of a half of an hour
of comfort everywhere
the dark engine off
the van's quiet hold
an eight-year-old boy
waking up as a pharaoh wakes
soft skin covered in flowers
the most open part of a world
on which you are stalled
indistinguishable little-boy life
without humor for many minutes
tulip heads viciously plucked
and thrown into darkness
a young boy exercising flowers
to an uneven end of the van
steadiness and quietness
taking him over
undaunted balance of childhood
from which tulips grow and fall
and in the front seat a sleeping man plain

divorced three-quarters full of the desire to be okay
father of one young boy lover of electronics
proud owner of two cheap walkie-talkies
which in the dark highway full of night
sound angelic in a modern way
angels descending on Wyoming
with wisdom their walkie-talkie ways
slipped into that paternal lap
a door swung open
coldness wind dampness evening
fluorescent light pooling
onto the abandonment of the road
and the boy
young thumping run
from the van
to the dark waiting shoulder
the empty straw field beneath him
the darkness settling around him
the world quiet
heavy and common
a familiar feeling
doing this so many nights in a row
you become part of the night
relaxing leaning into it
the dreamy-eyed very plain
not remorseful man begins to think
in a truly non-judgmental way
about the drifting
his life does about moving
and moving's effects
but also about his life's wonderfulness

about the friends within it and the coffee
the assuring electric voices
(by which he must mean the sound of tires
the hum of engines) clarifying the validity
not only the validity but also the respectability
of living a life as he does
not pushing too hard
but paying attention when attention calls
and when it does not he does not when it sings
in a loud operatic voice he listens
until it is over and when it cries
gulping childish cries
for hours he listens
until the crying ends a city
just twenty minutes away
its warm comforting coffee waiting
for a man age forty-two
youthful unexaggerated forty-two
lap full of walkie-talkie
speaking softly
becoming near
becoming distant
in instants a van
a washed-out voice saying
"Superman come in
come in Superman"
miracle of modern technology
trying its hardest to bring
fathers and sons closer together
sons singing "Superman come in come in Superman"
"this is Wonderboy Wonderboy wondering if you can hear me"

wondering about coming in wondering about the barely audible
coming in I must be doing a tiny bit of nothing in the night
a van full of tulips moves steadily
in and beneath the darkness
the walkie-talkie unnoticeable
in a man's numbing lap
the Wonderboy
like just another handful of darkness
hurled into darkness
wake of a white van
soft bulb of lights
before headlights
tulip comet of fatherhood
progressing with time
in the perfect condensed darkness
the sounds of "Superman come in come in Superman"
sounding a tiny silence beneath tulips
monstrous tulips leaning over the memory
of a child who despite all his present ineffectuality
is a Wonderboy a source concerned with his destiny
breaking through the underbrush of night
a van moves fragrant and simple
the road no different
the migration of adults upon it
as if an extra sense led them to it
they would find it even at night
a van full of tulips
moves through Wyoming.

ABOUT THE DAYS

Open moments of winter
are two, your brown eyes
darkened departing your
brown eyes nothing but
Europe but winter will do
for the window opens
and the arm extends
from it saying January
make me cold as you must
and the body is dedicated
to you full of armfuls
of you, that is two,
how it was with you and
how the winter was and
how the winter was within it.

Ecstatic and returning

                                      is the message

is the message you leave on my machine

telling me something about

                                            going ahead

                                   and stopping and

                                      going ahead

  In helium you become all high

and float away and in listening

you are delayed as if

by the wrist you are held but go

alas, nor rhyme nor form nor old

English ways could

                              but drift

         and cannabis

                  and dust lifting

from the floor

                        Will a beautiful woman

make everything right? Can she accommodate

me in her princeton well liked?

                    (and move on)

Light as a jet plane upward you could
not reach my mouth even once. She would
change she would not stop, anything, may you
may you sleep in the big state where
your mother will take you to get better
and may you get better there

ecstaticness

go away and be ecstatic on someone else's
time, here among friends do please let me be,
let me be not the feather I was, floating into bars,
inde inde independent as daylight, ok with that
love we've been giving each other, do not
want anything from yourself tonight

ecstaticness

is gone. (Her mother's arm did all the
brutal things, all the weighty helpful
things. Was nutrition. Was consent.
Was the hard pillow beneath the head
that would not drift off as the arm
held it still, would not move)

and in the choppy water
the cold water, the men pushed
deep into the Hudson with their oars,
and through it came slowly toward land
and once upon land took their boat
to safety, and once to safety stretched
their legs, thought heartening things
about the weakness of their legs, the
lifelessness of ground.

There is someone in her life that stops her
from loving me and no one in the vice versa
of my life. So I go to William Carlos Williams
say, you're a doctor, what should I do
about this woman and her trip to Florida
her life's lack of entanglements in mine
and the beaches. I'm such a hardass
I probably wouldn't even move there
for her, but for the beaches
　　I would move to Oklahoma
　　　　and so persist, to the newspapers
　　with your story, but to her

Resurrect the god of two bodies not knowing
each other all night. Resurrect the comfort
of morning's still obliviousness.

　　　　and the haiku of japan, the attractiveness
　　　　　　of ancient egypt, and paterson on the boardwalk

　　　　　　of america, and pigeons, do you
　　　　know anything worth writing about

　　　　　　　　yes I do, yes and no.

New Orleans trumpet sounds blowing out.
Sarah in the swimming pool. Me in the living
room. Michael impatient with people, in Florida
I do things that make me cry all the time.
Coming back from vacation.
Remembering passion. Nodding equivalently
on the verge of something for years.
Thin body in summer, stationed, sweating,
Sarah swims from the trumpet so smooth
Days project themselves independently
Summertime, and the living is easy
The fish are jumping and the cotton is high
You are rich You are good looking
Hush little baby, don't you cry

Geniuses throwing themselves
in front of subway cars

Montauk with its cold waves
its quiet waterfront

Your initial sense is that things here
are desperate, desperate

                                    Jones Beach
                                    Long Beach
                                    Fire Island

That people want to get away
can be read in their faces
                                              offer Diana
offer her some sort of love
is what my all-too-small heart is saying
though I don't love her, offer

Diana spread like a newspaper and flew
to Coney Island and from Coney Island flew
like a newspaper away

                                    Jones Beach
                                    Long Beach
                                    Fire Island

———

And when she was gone
it is just as they say
she was gone

Are geniuses everywhere?

This is why I press my lips
to you because of questions

Bruised and seeking perfection
there are hundreds of us on every corner
    ample discordant upsetting

  in lieu of romance, lust
  in lieu of passion, passion atomic
  in lieu of time continuous and trajectory apparent
  a whistling astronomy of things to do for forever

I came here to kick ass and take names
what are the rest of you here for

I mean I came here for all of you
  among whom love's odds increase
    what are you all here for

    in lieu of the body's heroic burning in plenty
    is its weakness aflame

Did you notice how we are all doing pretty poorly?

I said half deadpan half realistic

Embrace me New York
    your many, your tiny magic,
      embrace me

and she did, naked and perverse
and after knowing me for minutes
she was distant and in my arms
exposed, and not by any means
the first

                    New York says
        do not regret, continue

It says prosper mighty anecdotal life

I am unhappy with everything
I do without you and ashamed
all over again thinking how
I was with you,
                    Us in a wooded Massachusetts fall
and the pulse of this place recognizable in my actions.

It's cold. It's cold. Sky over Brooklyn
don't rain, I have plans for my city today.
Make important promises to me. Lasting.
For not collapse inevitable. Declarations
of foresight on me bestow with continuity
in your nature. Brooklyn sky, has anyone
told you you're all I've got and you
just well up and cry cold Brooklyn rain
over everyone. Sky above Brooklyn I want
promises. I desire promises from individuals
strained to make such promises. Brooklyn cold
my smoke-filled chest buoys up in your waters.
To the extent we can fear the giant fears
coming to pass, I have feared them recently
and today's Brooklyn cold continued on
walking the streets toward the end
of the daytime, enjoying what you said
and your rare appearance departing.

Oh slow motion bed sheets in sunlight
(hung out to dry in tenement chorus)
and provocation (they dance like emotions
in this least important of years) It is 1955
or it is 1998 or it is another expectant
evening of blue
        when Rick says:

                        She's too young and too pretty
                        to be dealing with crap like that

    to mention her was something
it was very observant of him
        and of her what can be said
                but that she goes
                just wherever her ass takes her
in which we realize there is something valiant
far sooner and more clearly than we realize
        the desperation, 1955 returns
    to our conversation because he said her lips
and the sheet returning to our tenement courtyard
because it is still damp returns to our conversation
because of how it implies serenity in an age
of mechanical wisdom and Rick returns out of respect
for wise well-thought-out answers

                                        I am not right
        for you, though I think about it all the time

                                (pearls)

pearls are drastically retro
and yet there is nothing better
for the punctuation of contemporary
                                        beauty
                        he said, accessing a vanity for himself
        as well, and did I mention how she got up and left
or him, or the courtyard or the bare tenement wall
                fading in sunlight a bath of sunlight
                        and did I mention him

This morning there will be no leaning over the water
or not enough, your hand in the water, no falling off
the bridge over which even Hart Crane could not throw himself
today. It is slight, this giant river, and overwhelming
his friends say, "here, the hand-held dagger of sunlight
for your heart" and we have them too for our own hearts
to be virtuous on a cold day and to be virtuous on a day
like today the orthodox rest and resting bring January
with them wherever they go and they go so slowly
over the Williamsburg Bridge, they are seductive, join us
in the season we bring with us everywhere, arm in arm
and into the city they said, "slowly, slowly you will become...
a blessing at a time, one for the cold water and one
for the tumbling in, postponed, and one for never touching
the water again, for floating into the sky again, the arms of heaven
are arms "amen" the men of heaven are men "amen"

> drop your weapon
> > into the reflective pool
> > of our love

> devise no secrets
> > for the downfall
> of others today

> > construct no barricade
> > > of sin that will break
> > > the hearts of others today

that broke the heart
of another, and do not break today
the heart of even one more

Elohenu Elohenu Elohenu today love
arrives on its own "Elohenu" "Elohenu" "Elohenu"
means God God God come into my wanting come into
my celebration come into my wanting again, and the sea
with no reason, swells, and the river, from it, grows
and falls and the bridge over which even Hart Crane
could not throw himself today, draws cars and trains
and cars and trains and cars and trains over
the water, calls them deep into the hapless city.

To climb the many flights
to one's apartment without optimism.
The woman pushes at both sides of her skirt,
as Paul Blackburn reads, from the inside,

> "I fled New York somehow,
> it's all hers now . And cold ."

and to get to the gray silent treatment
after putting in all those hours at work is unfair.
And to rest in the grayness compounds,
from which smokers are born
and in grayness exist
yet wish to leave their city
and their grayness
and their . . .

> Dear theoretical loved one,
> In parting I give you everything
> Entire common dining masses
> Sexy walkers late for work
> Brooklyn bobbing in its own independence
> and prosperity, big city, isn't it

clouding up already
for my own demanding clarity
demands a departure dramatic
as the man put it
"and cold"

What cabin expels the memory of you
so poetically, and for nature?

What lake demands the venture rejuvenating?

I rush home every day
to fill you with my smoke
and so don't leave
and here "and cold"

BLOCK ISLAND

The bathtub is not big enough
and with your hand you softly
splash water over you
light relaxing itself
on the floor
the basil wind
of summer, your papers acting
like unconcerned domestic animals
spread across the kitchen
coming home to that
love full house
of a year ago
a year ago
and now
them all picked up
and opened and closed and opened
and a year la la la a year
is just another secretary in sneakers
getting sun getting sun
and one could stay all day
in one's quiet room

soft undisturbed loneliness
tea the gentle need of house plants
an ancient Chinese poet
once wrote a story about how
for more than a month
without a job
I would leave the house
walk down the street
the willful composure
of my settled home
calling me home
where I would praise it
inherently tranquil
to leave and
to leave again
with some other reason in mind

❋

I have a lot of directional-going within me
a lot of dark confused lack of control
heartfelt vibrations of the mind
flat outstretched part of your hand
holding something down, your hand

there and the ride home
held down all day

while driving you say, "there
the blue blue calligraphy
of a blue balloon let go."

⁂

Dull heart,
you are out of breath.
One day you are hoarse
one day you promise to do everything
silently, and are hoarse again.

Arthur let go
his parents passing away
meaning everything
and passing away
one year
and four years later
there is no one to have tea with
to sit with

        A bird
            is alive in my building.

a birthmark which I mistook for a drop of blood
on the body during an affair and proud
of myself for working you that hard
and specific

cries
contradicting myself
with the desire for punctuation
with the desire for plausibility.

Love, you are dull
you are simple
unacceptable incomplete
you rush places
sway crowds
act mean
and low
and honest
every chance you get.
Come, take me away from this.
I have romance for you.
I have passion for you.
I have the shrill sounds
of a bird caught in your hallway.

❄

How much love
          moves around
                              without sound
                    and then the sound
              of lips through drywall
      going about their loving of someone else

"surprise doesn't come from waiting
around for it"
but something must
I will let you know

Sailboats
their sails
full
water, the wake its water
a ferry returns to the island
water, its wind its wake
a ferry asleep in the sunlight
full
their sails
sails

How much love
moves around
without sound
and then the sound
of lips through drywall
going about their loving of someone else
"surprise doesn't come from waiting
around for it"
but something must
I will let you know

                birds
                        escaping
            rooftops, the ferry slowed
                itself without sign
        in the water, water lapping
    handsomely against it, the ferry
    resting for minutes and within that time
    that time never ended,
                        the end
                            the birds
                the ferry
            the rooftop

    How much love
            moves around
                                without sound
                        and then the sound
                of lips through drywall
        going about their loving of someone else
                    "surprise doesn't come from waiting
                around for it"
                        but something must
            I will let you know

                        ❊

    Leave home
    with all your stuff
    your girlfriend at work

returning to the knowledge
that you are gone
because she left you
in heart her fondness
and love (caring) still there, but left
in heart passion and the other two off somewhere
cramped in a house the size of a fish can
and not particularly unhappy with it and me
always repeating what you say
and what everyone says
because I am distracted just not listening
distracted distracted
                        Soon she will
be attracted to everyone

                  so light, blame
                        is as unimportant
                        as a second orgasm

                                    I just
feel attracted to everyone
                          "We know"
is what we said in a way because we know
and will not ever see her again we will not
ever see you again and I love you to us
is what she says every time we see her
floating by like a let-go balloon
and I am answering questions all day long
not one of them you bawling over the loss
we can all feel you feel
                  not calling

—————

is perfect
unfortunately perfect
because I will be distracted
                    by the sound of a woman
                            floating behind you
        the moon
looks directly into your eyes
            and you into it
        and there is always a third person with us

                        You need my love
and I give you a poem, you need my understanding
            and I give you the criticism
        of love's temperature always changing
        and never returning
    though some people will tell you
    that everything returns
                acting this way
        is people's way of being
    distracted me
                        the sour look of her
                no longer in love face
                not infatuated, worse I say
        is that you just keep longing for her
    stop longing for her

Do I understand, of course I understand
Do I know what it feels like, of course I know
Do I fall into the same traps of loving
everyone else falls into

Please, when this is over, tell them all
how unacceptable I am on the telephone.

Did you see my eyes darting. Did you hear me
repeating, yes every word you said.

I care that she left you.
I want to hold you very tight because of it.
But if you call, what will I do.
Listen and then it won't be enough.
Talk and then it won't be enough.
Floating dismayed twenty-three year old
                    bright red balloon
              land back in my friend's yard
                    is what you would never do

              enough

                                   enough

       enough

                    enough

you can see the birds
and me, I approach progress like this:

＊

The ferry backs away from the dock before landing.
It is good to be tentative, at times to feel tentative
This is just my opinion but
And to be young at times is good as well.
Flying off to weddings. Going places.
Every time I go down town
the ferry is landing or landed, emptying
or emptied. Every time I buy lunch
Every time I smoke   Probably you do things
that make you tired and you do things that make you sick.
Some day I will go to Paris every time I want to go to Paris.
Romantically I will die young in front of crowds
my childless body spilling out onto the pavement and then
I will get up and do it again.
One day I will do it for a beautiful woman
and away into history we will float together
where I will do it again for her in private.
This dying, it is sort of pleasureful. It is
like a puppet show. Caress and gesture.
You are a wonderful little show for me
she will say to me and I will die again dramatically
into the streets. What about the desire?
Thank God. Go places. These arms, what about them?
Fall lovingly lovingly, blue paint over Sarasota,
Clearview. History, fabulous history, tell it like it is.
Say flooding, say flooding, say ebb, and say tide.

✳

Did a bird
get loose
in your house
like the high key of a piano
ting tinging a song
off your walls and windows?

Welcome to the electric mind
of I am and want to be
twenty all day long.

My tongue met winter
on your tongue
and we hit it off
like ice or the exchange
of tiny quarters.

✳

We begin to rest in the daytime
in every time thin sheets the wind
blowing over them and us

Without saying naked or being obvious
I have made myself tired

                              Your presence

somewhere else is the sad warm thing
blowing around my room.

———

＊

Here in the middle of the middle ages
young men jump off boats

                tall and something
   free-spirited says do not photograph me
    my body is a carnival that tans
      and does not accept praise
  as the jet skis swarm their good-byes
around the ferry
     for a quarter-mile
   then taper off
individual random acceleration

               nakedness

     is as present
   as it ever was
     in public
    and some men discourage it
 by working in the day
     and fishing at night

This is how good
our country is getting

        summer
     stopped providing love
   to people years ago
   and they do not complain

large-mouth bass
large-mouth bass

I love a woman
        and a woman loves me

But love's successful
        infrequently

❄

Carelessness lighting up in their eyes
                        their bodies twisting
                the air the water
                        risk splashed against stomachs
        light through salt is perfect
to start you crying
        these boys in black sneakers
                falling through the daytime
        a young woman was born
        with wonderful pearly eyes
        so much they noticed it at the beginning
and the doctor said congratulations Mr. and Mrs. So-and-So
        you will have no trouble finding her a husband
        and as far as almost everyone was concerned
        her black hair clinched the deal
                but you still have to make it through high school
        and boys' bodies burn for such insignificant things
and she walks by one unnoticed time after the next

thinking I want boys to jump off piers
their skin a certain dried by sun softness
and land in me and does not blush
thinking this because this is what she thinks.

❋

Someone said we sweep women off their feet
when we feel this way. I met a woman and

All summer long I became dark freckled and handsome
dark freckled and handsome.

❋

The water was up to the jetty, deeply
The water lapping over, swells, deeply
I dove into it as it came near, near to you
my deep blue water, a body floats
its dream says I am heavy and light all at once.
Some day there will be the night in which we play.
Love is bobbing with the unconcerned weave of the current
and particularly I feel this way when I am around you.
Sometimes, in the night, the earth will change for a man
the earth will open up for him and his belongings.
When I am out in the world and the air does its little displacement
with my body, I think of you moving with the horizon
in and out of view.

Off into the atmosphere
music goes there
classically
strings
dispersed melodies
the stars
and behind them
the stars
connecting up
the deeper and deeper
of what we wish for
does not end
and she seemed to be getting the picture
of what it is to be here
giving me a bite of her pancakes
and cranberry juice
which they have here
and do not have
to tell you
that in your eyes
the freckles lightening
as your shoulders become arms
I believe I see
the traditional town life
of the 18th century
a sense of work
and ground that is
not here with us

now in a time
that just is
what it is

Do you know
what I think?
I think money should never be the issue
nor should age.
Today pack all things quantitative
onto the ferry and send them away. Notions of fullness
and emptiness overloading and sinking it. One night
we took off all our clothes and swam out to the wreck
whatever current it was kept pulling us down shore
seeing and losing sight of it (giant it) and us just

The cold water
The salt water
The light mist
The unexpected exaggerated
Love, let's go back. The kids are sleeping.

❋

An hour. A few minutes. I'll wait for people, the sun, a wind
can just like that sink the jetty in dark expectant waters.

✼

the yellow flowers
little actually grass
spread gap-toothed
across the hill
and down at the water
the jetty covered over
disappearing and reappearing

Danica said:

a virtual hurricane
of small islands scattered
along the coast

uninhabited and inhabited
but still so quiet
you are pushed against it
the water is active
for swimming
and for falling asleep by

Cold night
there in the middle of summer
dreaming of the warm body
of one's new lover
the clouds open up
directing you to awake awake become part of the day
you rise and in your home the radio
is playing news from America

there is so much between home runs that disappears
resting a useless out-of-breath rest on the couch
glass doors
salt
summer light
the meaning of the day before
when you went into the water
for a guy you didn't know
helping him wrestle a twenty-pound striped bass
so wet, our mouths hung open
and the hanging tail of your shirt
and whatever love
we had been afraid to go searching for
appeared present and accessible.

❋

It rang and rang generously welling up in me
pouring over my edges, rang and drifted off
drifting off if you pick up the phone
I will overflow and love you forever
tell you I'll love you forever, friends
can do this, bear down on one another with emotion
and when it is too much the phone will
just ring and ring and ring and flatlined
by the woman I stood there thinking
how mean she was and how much I wanted her
not to be that way and how much my wanting
would never pick up and you once said I'm not

going to leave until we figure this out said
I won't leave until we figure this out.

❅

In what you are doing, you are falling in
one-sided love, and falling out before lunch
and in before dinner, and out before nightfall
and sleeping alone and waking to morning
with morning so good

                               caught up in yourself
the way you go swimming, you dive off the jetty
 and into the cold.

                          We sing to your singing
the water is leaving, you love it and trying to let it
    and go.

                I said to you softly
your face tilting that way, I wanted no more
than the little I wanted. I said to you softly
and spoke to you this way, drifting off easy
    away from the shore.

❅

Temporary lightening
of the chest, the eyes
you dazed by the sun

———

and lifted to the sky
a kite covers the glow
and glows like aluminum
and uncovers it.
                    I ran,
out of breath, and ran
again. We have
the sun, we have
                    the sun
and when we sing
we feel so young.

                              ⁎

Good-bye perfumed touch of summer
the light was so responsive
finding gold and green in beach grass
and purple and white the wild roses
and time in the night to get lonely
before sleeping and acceleration
for sparrows and motorcars
when they need it and rest
to your breath the addition
of catching one's friends
up on one's new life is this plus that
equals something I expected to be different
more passionate more fragrant and
willful, more open-mouthed sweet-lipped

＊

and there was the ocean
   which came from beneath us
our lives just floating there
   and we watched them floating there

Joshua Beckman was born in New Haven, Connecticut. His first book, *Things Are Happening*, was published by the American Poetry Review in 1998. He presently lives in Staten Island, New York, where he edits 811 Books.